ANIMAL IDIOMS

Monkey See, Monkey Do: Do Monkeys Copy?

BY MARNE VENTURA

CONTENT CONSULTANT
JULIE LINDEN, PHD
INSTRUCTOR OF ANTHROPOLOGY
SUNY WESTCHESTER COMMUNITY COLLEGE

Kids Core
An Imprint of Abdo Publishing
abdobooks.com

abdobooks.com

Published by Abdo Publishing, a division of ABDO, PO Box 398166, Minneapolis, Minnesota 55439.

Printed in the United States of America, North Mankato, Minnesota.
102021
012022

THIS BOOK CONTAINS RECYCLED MATERIALS

Cover Photo: Ryan M. Bolton/Shutterstock Images, cover
Interior Photos: Monkey Business Images/Shutterstock Images, 4–5; Shutterstock Images, 6, 10, 26, 28 (top), 28 (bottom), 29 (top), 29 (bottom); Ludmila Ruzickova/Shutterstock Images, 7; Volkova Natalia/Shutterstock Images, 9 (gorilla); Eric Isselee/Shutterstock Images, 9 (chimpanzee), 9 (gibbon), 9 (capuchin), 9 (vervet), 9 (ring tailed lemur), 9 (sifaka); Gudkov Andrey/Shutterstock Images, 12–13; Vincent St. Thomas/iStockphoto, 14; Dirk M. de Boer/Shutterstock Images, 16; Natures Moments UK/Shutterstock Images, 18; Paula Photo/Shutterstock Images, 20; Simon Dannhauer/Shutterstock Images, 22–23; Lisa Crawford/Shutterstock Images, 24

Editor: Christine Ha
Series Designer: Katharine Hale

Library of Congress Control Number: 2021941240

Publisher's Cataloging-in-Publication Data

Names: Ventura, Marne, author.
Title: Monkey see, monkey do: do monkeys copy? / by Marne Ventura
Other title: do monkeys copy?
Description: Minneapolis, Minnesota : Abdo Publishing, 2022 | Series: Animal idioms | Includes online resources and index.
Identifiers: ISBN 9781532196690 (lib. bdg.) | ISBN 9781644946480 (pbk.) | ISBN 9781098218508 (ebook)
Subjects: LCSH: Monkeys--Juvenile literature. | Monkeys--Behavior--Juvenile literature. | Copying--Juvenile literature. | Animal instinct--Juvenile literature. | Idiomatic expressions--Juvenile literature.
Classification: DDC 599.82--dc23

CONTENTS

Little siblings like to copy their older siblings.

CHAPTER 1

Stop Copying Me!

The Tran family was about to eat dinner. They sat around the table. Dad handed Amelia a plate of food. Amelia said, "Thanks! You are the best cook." She took a big bite. "Yum!"

Sometimes people copy others they look up to.

“Thanks!” repeated James, Amelia’s little brother. “The best!” James took another big bite. “Yum!” he said.

Amelia frowned at him. She slammed her hands on the table. “Stop copying me!”

Monkeys and apes are some of the smartest animals in the world.

James giggled. He slammed his hands down too, yelling, “Stop!”

Mom and Dad laughed. “James likes to do whatever his big sister does,” said Mom. “It’s a case of monkey see, monkey do!”

What Are Idioms?

An idiom is an expression that is often used in a certain language. It usually means something other than the words that make up the idiom.

Monkey see, monkey do is used when a person copies the actions of another. It usually means the person copying does not fully understand the reason for the behavior.

Monkeys are mammals that belong to the **primate** group. Other primates include humans, apes, and lemurs. Primates are good at thinking and learning. They have hands that grasp. Many can climb trees and move on the ground.

Humans' Closest Relatives

Chimpanzees and bonobos are the primates most similar to humans. About 98 percent of human, chimpanzee, and bonobo DNA is the same. DNA is the material inside a living thing that determines how it looks and functions.

Types of Apes and Monkeys

Great Apes

Examples:

-Gorillas

-Chimpanzees

-Humans

-Orangutans

Lesser Apes

Example:

-Gibbons

Monkeys

Examples:

-Capuchins

-Macaques

-Spider monkeys

Lemurs

Examples:

-Ring-tailed lemurs

-Aye-ayes

-Sifakas

There are many types of primates. Great apes include humans, chimpanzees, bonobos, gorillas, and orangutans. They have larger brains and bodies than other primates. There are more species of monkeys than of apes.

A mandrill is a type of monkey. At 32 inches (81 cm) tall, male mandrills are the largest living monkeys in the world.

People often call apes monkeys, but that is incorrect. Apes are smarter than monkeys. Apes do not have tails. Monkeys do. Apes are built to swing through trees on branches. While monkeys also swing, they often run across branches instead. Chimpanzees and orangutans are apes. Capuchins and baboons are monkeys.

Is *monkey see, monkey do* an accurate idiom? Do primates really copy? For the most part, they do. Copying is a trait found in many types of primates. For some, it may be an **instinct**. For others, it is a learned behavior. Copying can help primates learn, survive, and form social bonds.

Explore Online

Visit the website below. Does it give any new information about apes and monkeys that wasn't in Chapter One?

Differences between Apes and Monkeys

abdocorelibrary.com/monkey-see-monkey-do

Copying helps some animals recognize others in their social group.

CHAPTER 2

Apes and Copying

Not all animals imitate others. But humans and many primates do copy. Scientists have found that apes copy both humans and other apes.

Chimpanzees use tools in many ways. They may use objects to get food or water, clean themselves, or fight.

In one study, researchers gave juice boxes with straws to two groups of chimpanzees. The first group dipped their straws into the juice boxes. Then they pulled the straws out and sucked on the ends. The second group sucked directly through the straws. The first group soon realized the chimpanzees who used the sucking technique got more juice. They switched to sucking through the straws. The chimpanzees found the best way to use a tool by copying.

Chimpanzees also copy for other reasons. A scientist found an older chimpanzee with a unique way of drinking. She dipped her arm into water, then licked her arm hair. Her children and grandchildren all drank the same way.

In another example, an adult chimpanzee hurt his fingers. Instead of walking on his knuckles, he used his bent wrist. The younger chimpanzees in his group started walking the same way. In these cases, copying helped the chimpanzees form social bonds with others.

Chimpanzees are very social animals. They travel together and protect each other.

Chimpanzees and Humans

A study at a Swedish zoo found that chimpanzees and human visitors enjoyed imitating each other. When chimpanzees clapped their hands, knocked on the window, or made kissing sounds, humans copied them. When humans made these gestures, chimpanzees copied them. This study showed that chimpanzees were not only aware they were being mimicked, but also enjoyed the interaction.

Researchers also compared copying in human children and chimpanzees in another study. They put treats in a box and showed chimpanzees how to open it. The directions had multiple steps, including two unneeded steps.

Scientists believe that when apes copy humans, they may be attempting to communicate.

The chimpanzees copied the researchers to get the treats. When the chimpanzees realized two of the steps were not needed, they skipped those steps.

Next, the researchers studied preschool children. Though the children realized there were unneeded steps, most still copied and did the extra steps. Scientists found that humans may have a stronger social instinct to imitate. For humans, imitation helps them learn new skills to share with others, such as making tools.

Chimpanzee Communication

Scientists have not yet been able to teach chimpanzees to use human speech. However, chimpanzees have been able to **communicate** with humans in other ways. Researchers worked with a chimpanzee named Washoe. She could use 250 signs from American Sign Language. She learned them by copying the researchers.

For humans, imitation is a form of social learning. It helps young humans connect with adults, as well as learn ways to survive.

In contrast, chimpanzees are more interested in **survival** and problem solving. They focus more on the goal than on specific actions. But in both humans and chimpanzees, copying helps them learn survival skills.

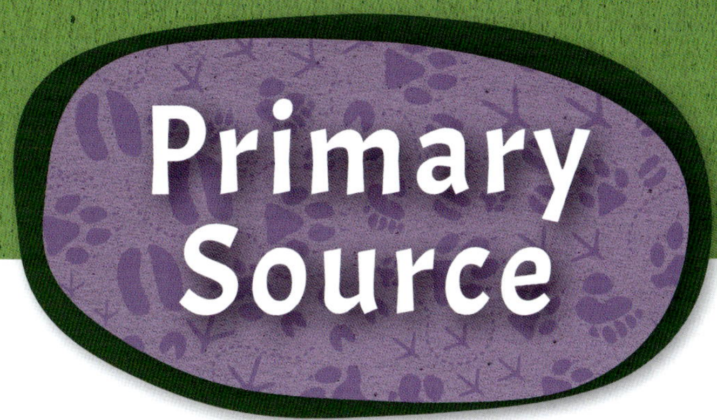

Scientist Wolfgang Köhler, who studied how apes copy, observed this:

> One ape, Grande, stands on boxes to reach bananas hung from the ceiling, while Sultan watches. . . . [Sultan] raises his arm in precise **synchrony** with Grande's grasping movement.

Source: Frans de Waal. "Monkey See, Monkey Do, Monkey Connect." *Discover*, 18 Nov. 2009, discovermagazine.com. Accessed 22 June 2021.

Comparing Texts

Think about the quote. Does it support the information in this chapter? Explain how in a few sentences.

Capuchins live in groups of 6 to 40 monkeys.

CHAPTER 3

Monkeys and Copying

There are more than 260 different types of monkeys. Capuchin monkeys are known for their intelligence and their use of tools. They form **social groups** and work together to survive.

Researchers have found evidence of capuchins using tools 3,000 years ago.

Scientists studied a group of capuchins in Costa Rica. The monkeys were given an unfamiliar fruit. The fruit was hard to open and eat. The scientists noticed the younger monkeys watched the older monkeys. They learned the best way to eat the fruit by copying.

Monkeys and Humans

In another study, capuchins were placed in three cages. They could move between the cages.

On one side, a human in front of the cage copied the monkeys' actions. On the other side, another human did not copy. The monkeys moved closer to the human who copied. When offered a treat, the monkeys preferred taking it from the human who imitated them.

The researchers think this kind of copying helps monkeys build social groups.

Ape and Monkey Actors

Monkeys' and apes' imitation skills have been used in human entertainment. For example, a monkey actor may copy human behavior for a commercial or movie. This takes a lot of training. However, some people do not think animals should work as actors. Some trainers do not treat their animals well.

Some baby macaques begin showing imitation behavior just a few days after being born.

Rhesus macaques have also been studied. Researchers found that these monkeys showed imitation behavior at a very young age. One researcher did an experiment with newborn macaques. The scientist stuck out his tongue. The baby monkey did the same. The monkeys also copied the scientist when he opened his mouth and smacked his lips. Scientists believe this is another example of how imitation is a form of social bonding and a way to learn behaviors.

So, is *monkey see, monkey do* an accurate idiom? Do monkeys really copy? Primates are naturally curious creatures who not only copy but also like to be copied. Imitating others is an important way for primates to learn behaviors, form social groups, and survive.

Further Evidence

Look at the website below. Does it give any new evidence to support Chapter Three?

Do Monkeys Really Do What They See?

abdocorelibrary.com/monkey-see-monkey-do

Monkey and Ape Facts

Apes and humans at a zoo sometimes imitate each other.

Newborn rhesus macaques were observed copying the facial expressions of researchers.

Young apes and monkeys learn by copying adult apes and monkeys.

Social learning, including copying, plays a big part in helping primates survive.

Glossary

communicate
to exchange information

instinct
a behavior animals are born with, rather than one they learn from parents or experience

primate
any of the mammals in the group that includes humans, apes, and monkeys

social groups
groups of animals that live and often work together to survive

survival
the act of staying alive

synchrony
two or more identical actions happening at the same time

Online Resources

To learn more about monkeys and apes, visit our free resource websites below.

Visit **abdocorelibrary.com** or scan this QR code for free Common Core resources for teachers and students, including vetted activities, multimedia, and booklinks, for deeper subject comprehension.

Visit **abdobooklinks.com** or scan this QR code for free additional online weblinks for further learning. These links are routinely monitored and updated to provide the most current information available.

Learn More

Klepeis, Alicia Z. *Jane Goodall.* Abdo, 2022.

Murray, Julie. *Acting Animals.* Abdo, 2020.

Murray, Julie. *Monkeys.* Abdo, 2020.

Index

About the Author

Marne Ventura is the author of more than 100 books for children. A former elementary school teacher, she holds a master's in education from the University of California. Marne and her husband live in California.